9 MISTAKES EVERY TORCH DISTRIBUTOR MUST AVOID

Shocking....

Distributors are Losing up to 37% Profit & they don't even know that

PRAISES FOR THE BOOKS

Really experience matters! Sachin ji has done a fabulous thing by writing this book. The issue that he has touched will be truly solved especially for torch distributors and dealers. His learning are presented in such an aligned way that not only torch dealers but even people in other industries will be benefitted. The 9 mistakes have been brilliantly identified and solutions to each one of them is beautifully explained in a simplistic way. Easy to read, this book is a must buy!

– Mr. Pradeep Rana (Advocate)
Founder, Pradeep Rana & Associates

Sachin Gupta ji's book '9 Mistakes every torch distributor must avoid' will be a great help for the people who are interested to join or start a new distributorship in any segment. The best thing about this book is that Sachin ji has listed 9 mistakes and explained them really well. The issues like how we are not able to connect with customers, how our strategy should differ from other marketing strategies etc. are well explained and in addition to that the solution is also provided in such a nice way. Great work Sachin ji!

–Dr. Shobha Gupta
Medical Director & IVF Specialist at Mothers Lap IVF Centre

The book '9 Mistakes every torch distributor must avoid' is a thoughtful and wise read for torch industry distributors and intermediates. Although I am not from the torch industry, yet we can connect the learning to other industries also. Due to the lack of knowledge, many distributors & dealers fail in the long run. But this book is a complete solution for them. They can now be able to save their profits by implementing the learning.

– Mr. Balraj Singh
Founder of FY Tech Industries, Bahadurgarh, Delhi

9 MISTAKES
EVERY TORCH DISTRIBUTOR
MUST AVOID

Shocking....
Distributors are Losing up to
37% Profit & they don't even know that

By

SACHIN GUPTA
India's Leading Torch Expert

PENDOWN PRESS

Powered by **Gullybaba Publishing House Pvt. Ltd.,**
An ISO 9001 & ISO 14001 Certified Co.,
Regd. Office: 2525/193, 1st Floor, Onkar Nagar-A, Tri Nagar, Delhi-110035
Ph.: 09350849407, 09312235086
E-mail: info@pendownpress.com
Branch Office: 1A/2A, 20, Hari Sadan, Ansari Road, Daryaganj, New Delhi-110002
Ph.: 011-45794768
Website: PendownPress.com

First Edition: 2021
Price:
ISBN: 978-93-91266-00-4

Layout Design: Pendown Press Publishing

Printed and bound in India by Thomson Press India Ltd.

Dedicated to
My daughter Ahana Gupta
who has driven me to make a difference
in this wonderful world
by her innocent belief in my strengths.
My Wife Preeti Gupta
Who has enriched my world,
shared her wisdom and supported me
in every phase of my life.

CONTENTS

FROM THE AUTHOR

The Torch Industry is a competitive industry. If you have chosen the distributorship or dealership of a LED torch brand, then you need to give your extra 1% to have an edge over your competitors. I have tried my best to relate my experiences with real business scenarios in each of the chapters, which would surely help the reader, understand the serious consequences of committing these mistakes. The idea of writing this book is to guide you a preventive course in conducting your business and to highlight some of the self-experienced solutions to prevent you from making the top 9 mistakes.

For the last 16 years, I have been a part of this LED Torch industry and have witnessed the ups & downs in this business. The mistakes that I have shared in this book are practically committed & rectified in the real world by reputed businessmen in this field but my hints & solutions given in this book can help you completely skip them for good. You just have to analyze them in context to your business before applying these solutions. Let your wisdom & character be the right judge!!

> *" The hardest challenge is to earn your consumer's loyalty and if you get that success will come to you."*
>
> **– SACHIN GUPTA**

PREFACE

> *"Your attitude, not your aptitude, will determine your altitude."*
> **– ZIG ZIGLAR**

In my field of work, I have to constantly deal with many torch distributors, dealers and suppliers. There are times when some of the business relationships with these distributors turn stronger and long lasting. But, in some cases, I have seen distributors ending their businesses within a short span of time due to business failure or severe losses in business.

Indeed, I have witnessed the good & bad journeys of many of my dealers & distributors during my career as a leading torch manufacturer. These drastic plunges in business profits and sudden end of their distributorship businesses used to boggle my mind. A piece of my mind and soul used to get jammed by such news and bothered me to understand the cause behind such mishaps in such a progressive torch industry.

It triggered an idea inside me. I decided to learn about their experiences, study the cause behind their failures in their businesses and, understand their obstacles in their career path. Finally, I started penning down all the issues, problems, challenges and mistakes that are causing them to lose revenue in such a lucrative sector.

This book has offered me a platform as well as an opportunity to save many people from becoming a prey to those mistakes and guide them in achieving business growth, better productivity and good customer base.

It could be a miracle reading for those who wish to start their career as a debutante torch distributor and a life-guard for those who are amidst ups & downs of their distributorship business and need something to survive or boost their business.

I sincerely hope that this book uncovers those insights that can help you avoid those common mistakes and provide you with all the effective solutions to come out of them.

Happy reading.

ACKNOWLEDGEMENTS

I take this privilege to express my thanks to my wonderful family i.e. my parents, wife and daughter for their unconditional love, support and encouragement. You all complete my world in all possible ways!!

I thank my inspiring mentors Mr. Rahul Jain, Mr. Akshar Yadav and Mr. Manuj Bajaj for coaching me to convert my studies & experiences into a guiding book. I am thankful for their motivation, time-to-time patient listening and effective suggestions. It has been truly very helpful.

I would like to thank Mr. Dinesh Verma, CEO, Pen Down Press and their entire team for publishing this book.

I would extend my heartfelt gratitude to Mrs. Kkanchi Goel, Founder-MK Writes India and Mrs. Pallavi Paliwal, Senior Content Writer, MK Writes India for screening & editing the book with utmost precision and in polishing the language.

I would like to sincerely thank my clients, friends and co-workers who have believed in me & my strategies and have supported me in my professional life.

Lastly, I will thank the Universe without which my conviction would not have converted into reality. The ultimate powers of the Universe helped me in my research and facilitated in completing my book and getting it published within a short span.

HEARTFELT GRATITUDE

Thanks for being such phenomenal readers and for taking out your precious time for reading this book.

I hope you have found this book a valuable read for your business and I wish my insights work wonders for you in terms of profit & productivity.

With this book, I have accomplished my goal to help people in my industry. My objective is to give my readers effective solutions to rectify those common mistakes that adversely affect the growth of their distribution business. I believe my efforts will help you prosper your business.

Your feedbacks, inputs and queries are always welcome and you can reach me at:

Globeam Radiant Pvt. Ltd.

E-mail: care@globeamindia.com

Website: www.globeamindia.in

ABOUT GLOBEAM RADIANT PVT. LTD.

Globeam is one of the leading torch brands in the torch industry of India. It offers a variety of supreme quality LED products and devices in different parts of India. Our lighting solutions & product collection deliver innovation, effectiveness and quality to our esteemed customers. We understand the needs of our rural and urban customers and offer them customized products to serve their needs & purpose. We believe in empowering our rural India through Globeam torches and lighting products.

About the founder of Globeam Radiant Pvt. Ltd. – Sachin Gupta

Sachin Gupta joined the Industry in 2006 to carve a niche as a leading torch manufacturer and put in all his hard work & dedication to achieve this goal. His determination led him to gain vast knowledge about technology and breakthroughs at the global level. The result of his hard work and leadership is the success of his brand Globeam in different rural and urban terrains of India. Today, he has truly brightened remote places, farms, villages, and households through his LED solutions and products. He has devoted over 15 years to the torch manufacturing business and has extracted his business experiences & understanding in his book which is an eye-opener for new and upcoming torch distributors and dealers.

INTRODUCTION

Hello friends,

In this competitive business world of the Torch industry, every distributor or torch Dealer is working hard to mark its presence and build its own place in the eyes of its customers. The question is how successful we are in our attempts and how well we have achieved our aim?

This book is a smart guide for those who wish to succeed but have not yet achieved success yet. I think you all want to know what is stopping you from achieving your goals, Isn't it?

In your passion to earn higher profits within a short period of time, you often make some serious mistakes which may result in immediate profits but could present serious consequences at a later stage. You may not realize them now but shall certainly regret them when you will realize them. So why wait for that time?

This book will help you identify top 9 mistakes beforehand and prevent you from losing about 37% of your hard-earned profit. It will make you analyze your wrong actions and help you correct them in time.

What if you fail to choose the right product for distribution?

Also, are you finding it challenging to stand before tough competition in your area?

Are you Tired of Warranty issues, Quality issues and finding the right solution of product for your customer ?

This book will highlight the cause of that mistake and ways to make the right move in order to save your business & any loss of profit.

Do you have a healthy and growing consumer base? If not, then the book will reflect what is making you lose your consumer base and the revenue. There could be some very essential factors that you ought to consider if you want to keep your consumer loyal. This book emphasizes on the ways to earn the trust of your consumers and build a long-lasting relationship with them. Also, **if you are not able to solve the concerns of your consumer then you must be doing certain things wrongly and it is time to correct them.** The book deeply reflects the importance of practicing market segmentation and not to assume all the customers in the same way.

In this digital era, where do you stand? Are you still following conventional and outdated ways of managing inventory and accounts? Inventory and accounts management are crucial parts of any organization and if you are making the mistake of mis-managing them then your business is in the danger of losing profits. This book shall open your eyes to the problems that may incur in the smooth running of your business if you have not adopted the latest technological practices of managing accounts & inventory.

It is not difficult to change but before that it is important to accept the mistakes and become willing to change. Read the book and explore the top 9 mistakes that can cause you to lose your profit percentage by about 30-37% and the steps that can be taken to rectify or prevent them.

MISTAKE-1

DON'T SELL ALOO, SELL SOMETHING NEW

If you keep on doing the things that most others are doing, you will keep on getting the things what's others are getting. When I spare some thoughts on the distributors, especially in the torch industry, it makes me worry at times to see the distributors sell what others are selling. Though it is good to go with the masses, at the same time, it takes away the opportunity from you to do something unique, something out of the ordinary, that will spell magic to your customers within no time and make you earn a recognizable place in the market.

Distributors, contrary to the popular belief, do not sell just the products. They provide engineering support, after-market services, play a central role to reduce costs, manage inventories, know the pulse of the market, and thereby create value for the manufacturers and customers.

When you sell a thing that has common presence (say, Aloo), you will be perceived as just another human being. No one will attach importance with your name. But, if you do an extensive research on the Market and become successful to explore a product that might have very big Consumption Capacity in a 100 km radius, you become able to monopolies your product, win praise of your customers and you become able to make your presence felt far and wide.

One of my friends' younger brothers was looking quite sad after he failed in the distributorship of water bottles. He had decided not to take the distributorship of any company, for he felt that the job of distributor itself is so unfortunate, that it is destined to fail. He said to me, "Bro, I did everything I could to thrive in this business, but I COULD not even survive. I think I was into wrong business. Distributorship is something that is destined to fail."

After giving him a patient hearing, I tried to calm him down, and said, "Goldy, we are not doubting your ability. We know you are more capable than both of us (me and my friend), but as much as I can make out you have become the victim of 'Problem of Plenty'. The distributorship of the products that was in your hand, was already within just the radius of a few kilometers. When everyone around you is a distributor of Aloo, the chances are very less that you will survive in this highly competitive market.

Have you studied the torch market before starting your distribution business? If not, then do it now. The first step before starting your own distribution business in the torch industry is market study and analysis. Try & understand the wants & needs of your consumer as deeply as possible. Understand your competition and your chances of success in choosing that brand & its product for distribution. It can prevent you from becoming the victim of failure by not choosing the already existing & highly supplied product. Moreover, you can prevent your business from losing around 37% of your profit by making the right analysis, choosing the right brand and selling a quality rich product.

So, never make this mistake of going behind the running products. They are trending and running because someone like you introduced those products in your market. Instead, you yourself can create an atmosphere where you can set the new trend in your market.

> *"Try new things and discover a new you every day."*
> **– SACHIN GUPTA**

You just need to identify a good product and a good company to work with and start nurturing it. It will take some months of hard work initially, but for long term profit and growth of your business, this is the magic key. On the other hand, this aloo selling may give you volume for some time but sooner or later you will end up in a situation of very little or no profit. Resultantly, the very enthusiasm to work more and work better, fulfil your dream will end, and you will find yourself cursing your fate.

So, the only solution to earn good profit and have sustainable growth for a long time is to explore a product that is unique and guarantees value of money.

After spending considerable years in the LED torch industry, I can name a number of things that a budding entrepreneur can choose for the distributorship.

MISTAKE-2

NEVER SELL LOW QUALITY PRODUCTS WHICH DO NOT HAVE A WARRANTY

Just take a glance on the advertisement campaigns, and you will find so many slogans like, "best quality products at dirt cheap price", "Brilliant-best quality at unbelievable price", **"*Aapke Zamane mein Baap ke Zamane ka daam*" (Price of your father's time).**

These types of slogans (appeals) are used in a variety of products and services, clothing, cosmetics, furniture, things of utilities and lots more. But, if the reports of marketing researchers are to be believed, these so-called mouth-watering appeals hardly find any importance or effect among the targeted consumers. However, these slogans give rise to a number of questions:

Do these too-good-to-be-true slogans really make the consumers believe that the prices are low?

Do consumers disapprove of the universal fact that high quality equals low price?

And the one-liner answer of the above-asked questions is that "the bitterness of poor quality remains long after the sweetness of low price is forgotten."

If you have made up your mind to sell low price – low-quality products, you are probably inviting a slow death to your business.

When I said this to my friend, who had been selling a low price, low-quality product and was quite happy with his phenomenal success, he became angry at me.

"You have probably gone jealous of my success. You are not able to stomach my rise and fame in my business. You think:

how come! How come an inexperienced & young person like me can achieve such a height in such a short span of time."

I knew he was a Power Drunk now, so I decided not to educate him further. But, soon my assertion started becoming true. The intensity with which customers had come out to take his products, went away with double of that intensity. Soon, he ended up as One Year Wonder.

By selling a cheaper and low-quality product, you are not only losing your reputation, but also losing your client base, **losing profit** and hence losing your business.

Torch Products with better quality and warranty earn word-of-mouth recommendation which in turn leads to rise in your sale. For instance: your product X is offering low prices, average quality & no warranty to the consumers whereas another brand's similar kind of product Y is promising better quality, one year warranty but comes at little higher prices. The possibility is that your product might draw the attention of many consumers who prefer value over quality but market study suggests that it will guarantee a short-span success only in comparison to product Y which will win better consumer reviews, recommendations, goodwill in the market and long term success. Product Y will surely take away all the chances of losing over 37% of your profit due to poor quality in comparison to product X. Think big, do better to get promising returns.

"A customer is never out of warranty; even if his product is."
– SETH GODIN

This is a trap of selling low quality and low-priced goods. By the time you realize your mistake, it will be too late for you to repair your image and save your business.

You might be thinking that, when a customer is asking for cheap and low quality what can I do ?

He may be unaware but you are not. Customers always ask for low prices until they don't have a strong reason to buy a costly product in front of a cheap product. Now it is your duty to prove the worth of your costly product so that customers can make a choice easily and buy your product.

Always try to sell good quality and with warranty products; those products may be little costlier than other products, but those kinds of products have the power to give you the right kind of momentum you need to generate growth.

"Product Quality always win
over the price of the product."

Remember, your profit is a by-product of your relationship with your customer. And you cannot have a good and healthy relationship with your customers by selling cheap and low quality products.

So, sell only good quality and if possible sell with warranty products so that your customer can have faith in you and always remember you as a trustworthy dealer.

MISTAKE-3

DON'T PLAY WITH TRUST OF YOUR CUSTOMER

The reasons I have chosen this topic as my chapter is that I fail to understand as to why a large number of distributors and dealers think that "Getting Trust is not as important as Getting Sales." Once good sales occur, trust will follow suit. But I argue exactly the opposite of what the Popular Proposition is.

Suppose you sell something by creating hooplas and tall promises through advertisements. Do you think these gimmicks are sufficient to Sell and retain your customer base? Just put yourself in that situation and you will be able to know for sure, what you will get in long-term. Say, you have purchased a particular mobile set as everywhere you see its hoardings, newspaper. Advertisements, TV Ads, etc. The job of these advertisements is over, the moment that mobile phone set comes in your hand.

Now, your loyalty with that company will come into play. If the product is what it was promised, well and good, but, if it's not, you will find yourself cheated, unhappy and rejected. Can there be any optimistic version of that situation? You better know the answer.

"Transaction is of Trust, not for the Money."
– SACHIN GUPTA

Distributors and dealers may not agree with me, but the fact of the matter is the transaction is of trust, not for the money. When trust is built, transaction of money becomes its natural outcome. When a customer comes to you, apart from the money, he also has trust that all the things that you have said (advertised) about your products are true, without any clause of disclaimer and he also holds a belief that if anything goes wrong under any unexpected circumstances (God forbids!), you will stand with him like a rock.

Trust is not something that can be well established quickly or through attention-grabbing advertisements. Relying on these publicity stunts is like making your customers relying on rain water that overflow on surfaces. Before long the water logging will go (your gimmick will come to the fore).

So, the crux of the matter is: Never try to Over Promise and Under Deliver. In fact, always try to Under promise and Over Deliver. Always remember: Customer is *sone ka anda dene wali murgi* (Your customer is the constant creator of your wealth).

> *"Give trust and you will get its double in return."*
>
> **– KEES KAMIE**

If you at all disagree with me, ask the companies that have lost their customers. Though they try their level best to repair their image, in the heart of their hearts they believe that a handful of advertisements can't undo the negative impressions about their companies. Very true, trust is not something to be forced down to the people's throat, nor it can be tricked out of the people.

A lost good name can never be recovered.

It is important to deliver what you promise in order to build a long-standing trust of your consumer in the torch industry. Follow these key steps and you will earn a loyal consumer:

a. **Be there to answer the queries & solve the problems of your consumer.**

b. **Offer them only good quality products to increase your market reliability.**

c. **Be transparent and honest to ensure them that you care.**

d. **Always put your consumer before your revenue.**

e. **Maintain uniformity and stability in your product & services.**

f. **Choose to sell only those companies' products which provide you spare & support.**

MISTAKE-4

NEVER ENTER INTO SELLING A NEW PRODUCT WITHOUT KNOWLEDGE & FULL CHECKING

1. **Don't sell brands without vetting its products**
2. **Don't go unaware in front of your consumer**
3. **Be the first user of your own product**

While sitting at my publisher friend's office, I questioned him, "How do you rate the profitability of your product (book), friend?

" If you don't believe in what you are selling neither will your customer. "

And his answer was, "Sachin, you happen to be the first customer of your product. If you are willing and ready to give the money that is printed on your book, you need not worry about its sale." And that thing, you know Sachin, will come through the comprehensive knowledge about your book. Unless you do not have good knowledge of the product, you cannot decide its

USPs, marketing points, and make it speak through the minds of its future customers.

There are numerous examples of this idea in our day-to- day life. Have you seen any cricketer predicting which party will win the next election, or Mr X predicting the IPL top scorer? Therefore, the bottom line is in order to make yourself heard, getting good knowledge about the things you are talking about, a must.

Wholesaler and dealer are supposed to be the answer to all the questions raised by the customers. If the customers find them unable to answer/mishandling some of their questions, they might drop the idea of taking the products at the last moments. Knowledge is power and if a wholesaler or dealer comes to know about its importance, he will definitely be able to reap big benefits in terms of sales. A good product knowledge will make you completely enthusiastic, generate excitement for the product, and enable you to explain to your customers about how this product is extremely necessary, and how it will bring positive changes in their life. Being best versed in explaining your products will provide you an edge over your competitors and selling will be as smooth as doing your regular activities.

What to Know About Your Products?

- Brief description
- How to use
- Servicing, warranty, repair information
- Pricing
- Why it is better than that your competitors sell

Why is product knowledge important?

As a led torch distributor or dealers, you can't make the mistake of half-knowingly selling any brand's product. As said earlier, think like a consumer and judge the quality of that product by knowing all about it. If convinced, then put your efforts in the right direction of sales-planning. Customer is not a fool but the most intelligent person whom you have to convince to buy your product. Knowledge about the product from the customer's viewpoint would help you relate the importance of that product to your target consumer. You will be able to confidently answer their questions and oppose their objections by providing them real evidence & case studies. Arm yourself with product knowledge for your consumer.

Do not focus on features

Most of the Dealers and Distributors of today make blunders by 'being talkative' on counting the features of their products, without being aware whether the customer is interested in it or not. Suppose, you have to sell a torch to a customer, who permanently lives in a plain area. So, you are not supposed to tell him that this torch is more beneficial for the people living in hilly areas, as this torch has a special feature of greater light in those areas. The bottom-line is: be specific, be customer-oriented, do not adopt one size fits for all approach. If you focus yourself on the customer that has come to your place, and explain successfully as to how your product will bring benefits for his specific needs, you will emerge as a very smart seller.

> *" The customer doesn't care about features.*
> *They care about solving their problems"*
> **– TRISH**

We have seen this in our torch industry, few distributors sell anything which comes to their way. They are not bothered whether the product is actually going to help their customers, or it is a useless fake product. It is not a good idea to sell anything just for the sake of profit; you may lose your years of hard work and goodwill with one wrong product.

This is actually a blunder. Before starting any business with any new company, always take your time, check the products, search the company details, how long the company is in this trade, etc. Try to go as deep as possible. The more you invest your time before starting, the easier it will be for you after the business starts.

Don't ever try to sell a product to your customer just for the sake of profit, unless you are convinced that the product is worth its value. Always try a new product at your end and if you feel the product is good enough with regards to its price then you can sell it with a lot more confidence.

A tried and tested product always gives you more customers as it has gone through several hands.

MISTAKE-5

5 MISTAKE OF FOCUSING ON PRICE AND NOT SERVICE

1. **Don't forget to 'satisfy your consumer' always**
2. **Don't rate just price of product but offer best consumer experience**

I often fail to understand the reason why the distributors and dealers of today focus only on price, and not on service. As a business owner, you have to decide whether to position yourself as a low cost, no frill player or as an above average cost charging, high value offering player. They take a short route of selling, and washing their hands off. And in turn, lose customers more rapidly than they build.

If you are ready to strengthen your relationship with your customers, by providing them after-sales service, letting them know about your latest product, sending them Birthday Wishes, making them feel that they are important for your business, make sure that the product they had ordered is available with you, you value their time and money, they will in turn build a mountain for your competitors. Your competitors will no longer remain competitors, as you will have taken over the market.

Contrary to the popular belief, sale is not the last step of doing business. In fact, it is the first step. The next steps that follow are providing follow-up contact and an effective way of dealing their queries. If you want to build a long-term relationship with them, win their loyalty and retain your customers, providing good after-sales service is a must.

I know a distributor at Koderma, a small place in Jharkhand. It is not a densely populated place. There are few shops near Thermal Power Station. People come there from far-off places. Madan is a distributor of mobile phones. He has a false impression that if he can sell his products at a cheap price, he can attract customers in large numbers. Initially, he did prove himself right. He indeed got good sales. But soon his shop got crowded with the complainants.

Customers started to jam his shop with their mobile sets—***Main itni door chalkar aata hoon, kabhi dukan band dikhti hai to, kabhi mobile repair karne wale nahi hote, jab se aapke yahan se mobile leke gaya hoon tab se dukhi hoon*** (I have to travel a long distance to come to your shop, sometimes I find your shop shut, sometimes your mobile mechanic remain absent, I am in great pain, since I purchased phone from your shop). There were complaints from all around. He would try to calm the customers with some already existing tricks like, "customer care par call karo", ***"aapne bachon ko de diya hoga mobile, unhone paani mein gira diya hoga, ab mujhe kya pata"*** (call customer care, you might have given your phone to the children, and they might have put phone on water, how can I help in these situations?), but soon his customers knew that Madam had failed to live up to their expectations, and subsequently he had to shut his shop.

Therefore, the need of the hour is to focus more on Customer Experience than to patting your back with "Low Price Gimmick." If you work well on your CX (Customer Experience), the customer loyalty of your Shop/Firm will always increase by multiple times. Convenient and painless purchasing with full faith on your products, that these are durable and perform as promised will work wonders for your products.

Simply put, you have to treat your customers the way you yourself expect to be treated as a customer and provide a sales and after-sales experience they prove too irresistible to experiment with any other dealer.

Give them a wonderful experience (related to products and purchase process) they expect, they will pay you the price that you expect.

Excellent customer service is the key to save 37% of your profit from falling down.

> *"Don't sell a product,*
> *Sell a world class experience."*
> **– SACHIN GUPTA**

The role of a 'really great consumer experience' is extremely important for the success of a torch distribution business. It is because he was happy with your after sales service and performance of your product. The first step is to focus on giving a rewarding service experience to your consumer and then, measure the consumer experience by conducting consumer satisfaction surveys & feedbacks, analyzing the rate of complaints received in a given period, and get their suggestions on product improvement. Ensure to delight your consumer at every touch point of service and keep adding value to your services over time.

If our distributors take by heart the notion "all that glitters are not gold" they will definitely be able to earn 37% extra profits.

MISTAKE-6

MISTAKE OF ASSUMING THAT ALL YOUR CUSTOMERS ARE THE SAME

"One size does not fit all"

It is important to understand the meaning of this saying as it is actually related to many businesses including our LED Torch distribution business. It states that every customer is unique and you should not make the mistake of treating them in one way. They all have different likes, tastes, preferences, purchasing power and consumer needs. As a distributor, it is important for you to take into consideration their unique demands and needs in order to offer them a personalized consumer experience.

Let me help you understand with an example. For instance, if we go out in Cafe Coffee Day, it is offering over 100 beverages with varying combinations as it has surveyed and identified the coffee preferences & taste of Indian customers and accordingly developed its chain of supply in India so that it can offer its customers a better experience of having coffee or other beverage than its competitors. Similarly, in the torch distribution industry, you also have to make a 3 step plan in order to meet your consumer's demands in order to give them the best consumer experience.

- **SURVEY & ANALYZE:** Put your time, money and resources in surveying the demands & requirements of your targeted consumers through collecting data via feedback forms, questionnaires, door-to-door interviewing etc.

- **SEGREGATE & SORT:** Now, that you know the demands & expectations of your consumer, it is time to divide them into groups. This way you will know the percentage of your target consumers, expecting consumers, occasional consumers and others.
- **STRATEGIZE & SUPPLY:** It's time to make right plans for marketing and selling. You will focus on the consumer's needs for the product and offer them just that as planned. Be attentive to your consumers' preferences and make sure to show your attentiveness in order to gain their trust.

It will help you in saving your precious time and prevent you from losing approximately 37% of your profit.

As a dealer you should not be making the mistake of painting all your customers with the same brush. If you keep a laser focus on different customers and their specific needs, you will be enabled to create more and more valued customers for your products. This, in turn, will turbocharge your sales and keep your loyal customers graph moving upwards.

If you're a torch wholesaler, for example, the profile of customers that buy Kissan torch in large quantities will be very different from those who buy dry cell torch or emergency lights.

Practicing market segmentation means separating customers into different groups with different promotions and marketing strategies to target them. Furthermore, you read earlier that it's possible to have different price lists for different customers

When you segregate your customer, you get an exact picture of the sales graph.

By segmenting customers, you are able to break down and track your sales in a meaningful manner and improve your sales prospecting and marketing strategies.

'Target the right audience and the right market' is a fundamental mantra for the business growth of torch distributors. If you have not split your audience based on their preferences, qualities, psychology and geography, then you will end up wasting your time, resources and efforts. Find the right market for your product, aim your marketing strategies accordingly, engage your target audience and get better returns on your investment.

This is the most common mistake in our LED torch industries. Generally LED torch distributors or dealers try to sell all the available products in his shop to all his customers, Resulting, it cost a loss of time & energy and hence loss of 37% of profit in LED torch & Emergency light industries.

MISTAKE-7

LOSING CONTROL OVER YOUR INVENTORY

Indian distributors and small retailers have still not yet adapted the ideal practices & technologies of managing their inventory. As a result, they sometimes don't know when the product is outdated or not in demand. In fact, sometimes shopkeepers hoard a product without actually checking whether the product is out of stock or whether it is still preferred by consumers. In the distribution industry, it is extremely important to keep track of the products you buy, store and supply. Also, you have to be aware of your consumer needs and demands in order to manage your inventory.

If you want your competitor's business to die naturally, just make him convinced that "Inventory Control is not an important thing at all in a business." As and when your competitor loses control over his inventory, he will **lose his profits** & business afterwards.

In fact, if you at all want to stay competitive in your business and **don't want to lose even 1% percent of your profits,** then inventory control is a must. This is simply because this single thing will help you maintain minimum inventory levels, deliver your products on time and increase your profits.

Unfortunately, a sizable number of wholesalers and dealers fail to understand the great importance of inventory control. They start thinking when they are asked as to how much quantity they have right now for a particular product. They still go with the manual inventory control.

Manual inventory control might help wholesalers to some extent, but as they scale high on sale, and thereby effective inventory control becomes the need of the hour, they can no longer become fully dependent on manual way of knowing their stock status, simply because human errors creep in.

I have got good reasons to believe that a more disciplined and structured inventory control is a must in order to achieve continuous growth in business and maximize sales through multiple channels.

Inventory Control relates to all important aspects about stock. It covers management and optimization of stock, and helps you to maximize your profit. If you have good control on your inventory, you will be better placed to judge the demand and supply for a product. In addition to these, inventory control will also help you keep a track of how much of your stock is sold, and whether the current stock is enough given the volume of orders or not.

How well have you managed your inventory?

Whether you are an emerging torch distributor or an established torch distributor, inventory control is a must to run your business smoothly & successfully. It requires constant monitoring and thorough evaluation. In the torch distribution industry, you are required to adopt suitable inventory planning methods that can help you in monitoring & controlling all the transactions starting from getting purchase orders to planning logistics & supplies. It is the best way to balance the demand & supplies in the business without any interruptions.

Importance of an effective Inventory Control strategy

If you avoid this major mistake in your business and keep a thorough check of the inventory periodically, then I guarantee you that you will not lose 37% of your hard-earned profit because:

- A well-managed inventory will help you avoid missed order fulfillment and lost business.
- A good control over inventory will remove the need for guess work, human error and frequent business disturbances and allow you to maintain the right quantity of safety stock.
- As and when your Inventory Control becomes effective, you get rid of out-of-date products, stealing of products from the stock and wear & tear of products.
- An effective Inventory Control will protect you from unexpected supply shortage, seasonal rise in demands and attain maximum customer satisfaction.

> *"Inventory is money sitting around in another firm."*
> **– RHONDA ADAMS, USA Today**

Take inventory stock count in such a way that it helps you make decisions about sales forecasts, stock sufficiency and stock re-ordering. This is the most expensive mistake which distributors make in our torch industry and lose more than 37% profit.

> *"Control over inventory means Control over profits."*
> **– SACHIN GUPTA**

They don't know about the current stock status. Many a time, we have observed that distributors reorder the stock just because they don't see the product in the front row and the product is in demand and they don't want to take the risk of short supply.

You need to be very alert about the stock in your hand, blind inventory status means blind business strategy.

Do regular stock takes for fast-selling items and monthly stock takes for slower items.

Finally, get a complete picture of your stock ins and outs with an inventory movement report. With this, you will know the exact quantity of incoming and outgoing stock for every item, in any location.

MISTAKE-8

USING PEN AND PAPER EVEN IN THIS DIGITAL ERA

1. **Don't forget to embrace the magic of digital record-keeping**
2. **Don't stay in pen & paper era, switch to digital era now**

I think business is primarily about maintaining records. Whether you make invoices, track the day-to-day business transaction, the transaction with your partners/consumers, the stock that you have, EMIs, GST details, amount of loan, advance given to your people, so on and so forth.

I have met several businesspersons having brilliant minds and excellent ways of doing business. But, what wonders me the most is there are some people, who have still adopted the decades- old way of maintaining record. They have not been able to think beyond pen and paper. They tend to have fat registers of almost every color available in the market, and put heading on its cover, like, GST, Invoice, Stock, Loan, so on and so forth.

If you also are still using the system of **'Bahi-Khata'** for maintaining accounts and registers for record keeping, then you ought to think again!!

Manual business processes make you slow in getting results and are not as efficient as operations done through electronic mode. The records maintained through pen & paper mode are often found inconsistent and are more incorrect which often mislead your strategies. They are definitely time consuming and require more of your manpower. It's time to evaluate your mode of operations now and review whether you are also facing the same issues in maintaining the **'Bahi-Khata'** system or not. You will find the answer yourself!!

Be it a small business or big distribution organization, you need to take a look around you. Digitization has entered in all business operations as it helps in their faster execution and adds ease to working.

It's time to move from **'Bahi-Khata'** to accounting software's, registers to computers, pen & paper to software applications in order to move along the world.

> *"If you turn a blind eye to technology, you cannot thrive in a business."*
> **– ANONYMOUS**

I just remember another example of Bathinda district of Punjab. The lady Divjot Singh, my close acquaintance, is running a beauty parlor. In 3 years, her reputation rose rapidly. Her beauty parlor became known for its excellent & satisfactory services. In marriage seasons, she remains so busy that she even forgets whether she had lunch or not. In the month of Dec., 2020, she applied for a bank loan, as she was willing to expand her business. The manager of the bank asked for the business transaction for the last three years. But she could not produce it as most of her business transactions were through cash only, and there was just a paper-pen format that could not impress the manager. Ultimately, she failed to get a loan from the bank. Had she maintained a record professionally, she would have been able to take hefty money from the bank and expand her business and thereby multiply her profits.

Have you switched from paper-based record-keeping to digital document management?

In the era of digitization and technology, if you are still following the ages old paper-based system of document management, then you are not making progress in real sense. It is not hard to make that switch now!! The torch distribution business world is moving at a very fast rate and in order to keep up to its speed, you need to integrate all the business information systematically in order to automate your daily flow of work. Follow the following steps to digitize your data and save the loss of profits by whooping 37%:

a. **Evaluate your data and accordingly capture it on suitable electronic software as available in the market.**

b. **Check out the inefficiencies you faced in pen &paper based systems and digitize those processes to manage them.**

c. **Integrate all the processes digitally and get data reports.**

Simply put, in order to compete with today's business challenges and requirements, it is important to adopt the latest technologies. Better technologies can improve the way of your business. To stay competitive, businesses should adopt technologies and upgrade it according to the modern world. The use of technology helps you see your products online, enables you to have a quick check on your stock, save your time, money and energy and empowers you to get away with registers for writing records as you can store your transactions in a database which is easily accessible.

MISTAKE-9

MISTAKE OF BALANCING CUSTOMER ACQUISITION AND RETENTION

1. **Don't choose one but focus on both: customer acquisition & customer retention**
2. **Don't forget to acquire as well as retain consumers**

Which one is better— getting customers or keeping them? Most of the time I keep asking this question and in order to settle this for good, I have decided to discuss this topic, in this chapter of my book.

Well, though these phrases are two sides of the same coin or the truth is that both are the two wings of a bird, they both are necessary for flight. In the absence of one, the motive of a wholesaler or a retailer for that matter will be defeated.

I often wonder why the so-called big-named stockiest, wholesalers and dealers focus only on customer acquisition and put retention on the back burner. But they make a big mistake by doing so. It is like trying to fill a container (achieve the target of maximum acquisition of customers), that is leaky (that does not have retention capacity).

Before I dig deep into Customer Acquisition and Retention, let me define the terms.

"Customer acquisition relates to the process of gaining new customers. This process includes attracting prospects and then making them convinced to take your products."

Whereas,

"Customer retention comes into play after customer acquisition. It relates to the process of engaging customers to continue buying products from your business."

So, now I think you yourself have understood the importance of these two. Gaining dollar is of no value if you keep on losing it at regular intervals, gaining knowledge on certain topic, subject is of little importance, if you cannot retain, teaching students are of little significance if they are not able to retain, purchasing certain amount of land is of no significance, if you are not able to retain, having a good health is of no value, if you are not able to retain. Simply put, acquisition and retention go hand in hand. This is as important as two hands for clapping, hand and mouth for eating, hands and feet for movement, so on and so forth.

So,What's the takeaway?

Every wholesaler, dealer should give equal importance to acquisition and retention and be equally attentive for both these aspects. It is simply because they both are the two faces of the same coin, sailors of the same boat, respectable members of the same family. In order to make your presence felt as a wholesaler, stockiest, dealer, etc. you must try hard to acquire news customers and that too without losing the existing ones.

In order to achieve the twin objective of customer acquisition and customer retention, you will need to develop a foolproof, practical marketing strategy that has the plans for both these aspects and exhaust all your resources to expand and retain your customer base, so that your business can enjoy steady and continuous growth.

Don't make the mistake of debating on this question: whether customer acquisition is important or customer retention? If you want to succeed, both are required. However, the focus may change depending on the needs and goal of the business as a torch distributor. If your goal is to grow & expand, then put your efforts on gaining consumers and in order to retain them for the long term, offer them best quality and excellent consumer experience. Once you have a consumer base, then focus should be on retaining them by reaching out to them via digital marketing & market segmentation (as discussed above).

If wholesalers and dealers of today learn to see both these terms, viz. customer acquisition and retention in totality, they will surely be able to save the loss of their 37% profit.

SUMMARY

This book revolves around the above key mantra and showcases the top 9 mistakes one usually makes as a torch distributor. These mistakes can cost them loss in profit, valued consumers and of course goodwill. So, If you don't want to lose your profit percentage by about 37%, then don't miss the chance of exploring the cause & effects of mistakes in this book. It includes a total of 9 chapters which focuses on things to avoid while running your torch distributorship business. Seek the solutions of some of the highly valuable questions now!!

What will happen if you would sell low quality torches or if you prefer being dishonest to your consumer for some percent of profit? Where would you stand if you choose to distribute a highly supplied torch product in the same market? What is the down side of mismanaging your inventory? What is the result of valuing price earnings over consumer loyalty? ..and more.

This book has provided simplified answers to complicated problems and highlights remedies to the mentioned top 9 mistakes. If you also want to excel as a successful torch distributor, then it would be smart to avoid them. The challenge is not easy and the path is not smooth, but read the book to get the right solutions. Happy reading friends!!

LET'S KEEP TALKING...

My objective is that this book is not the end of conversation, but the initiation of a long-term relationship.

I invite you to continue the discussion by joining me through social media channels mentioned below. Let's share our knowledge with each other and explore this unknown territory together. I also urge you to reach out to me for anything you would like to discuss about '9 Mistakes Every Torch Distributor Must Avoid'.

email: sachin.gupta@globeamindia.com

www.linkedin.com/in/sachingupta162/

www.globeamindia.in

www.ingramcontent.com/pod-product-compliance
Ingram Content Group UK Ltd.
Pitfield, Milton Keynes, MK11 3LW, UK
UKHW040028200726
13854UKWH00001B/422